Also by Don C. Nix

This Shimmering Life

Yearning for Transcendence

by Don C. Nix, J.D., Ph.D.

iUniverse, Inc.
Bloomington

This Shimmering Life

iUniverse books may be ordered through booksellers or by contacting:

iUniverse
1663 Liberty Drive
Bloomington, IN 47403
www.iuniverse.com
1-800-Authors (1-800-288-4677)

ISBN: 978-1-4620-5499-2 (sc)
ISBN: 978-1-4620-5500-5 (e)

Printed in the United States of America

iUniverse rev. date: 09/20/2011

Dedication

To Naya Pennington, healer, mystic, and ancient soul, who has graced our lives with her mind, magic, passion, depth and friendship, and who is a central pier in the unfolding of our sangha. With great love and appreciation.

Don C. Nix
Sonoma, CA
September, 2011

Contents

Introduction

We are evolving rapidly. It's a good thing, because we have exhausted this current phase in the unfolding evolution of our consciousness. For a couple of millennia, we have been wholly trapped in separateness. In the last 400 years, we also have been trapped in the mesmerizing material world. It has produced a worldview with a vision of the Cosmos as a dead, empty void, mechanically revolving like clockwork, with only a few bits of life, like ourselves, in it. This worldview has left us in desolation and despair.

Now things are shifting. All over the world, a new consciousness is emerging. Spawned in large part by the discoveries of quantum physics, this new awareness is moving us toward a re-ensoulment of the world. We are realizing that the Cosmos is awake and aware, and that livingness and consciousness are elements of Its primordial nature. We are realizing, incrementally, that the unfolding of the Cosmos is a single, seamless, creative event, and that we are the end product of that vast emergence. We are realizing that the story of the Cosmos, from the Big Bang to us, is our story, and that we are the Cosmos in human form. This awareness traces ancient realizations, literally thousands of years old. We are now recapturing Living Divinity, which exists all around us, and of which we are an integral part. It comes not a moment too soon.

1

I swim in unfolding Majesty,
while I'm doubting
my value and worth.
I'm suffused
with Shimmering Life,
while I'm pondering
my lack of success.
The universe flares Its wonders,
while I stew myself
in my fears.
Surely to God,
as evolving humans,
we can do better than this.

2

I am conscious.
I bow to You.
I perceive the world.
I bow to You.
I am alive.
I bow to You.
I'm on the Earth,
brought from the void,
having my human experience,
having my life.
I bow to You.
Every second of my life
there are one trillion interactions
keeping me on this planet.
I bow to You,
in wonder
and in gratitude.

3

Pay attention to your yearnings.
They are telling you where to go.
They're arising from your inmost heart,
from the deepest realm of Being,
to propel you on the pathway
that is waiting just for you.

4

I am here for just a minute,
walking the Earth as a man,
with full, rich senses
and a taste for experience.
I must wake up
and make the most of this,
this miracle of my life.
I must rise above the chaos
of fear and turmoil and strife.
I must open my eyes to see
the world that is coming to be,
and take my place
and act the role
that has been laid out
just for me.

5

Am I special on the Earth?
I think that I must be.
Something has brought me
from the void,
and crafted me,
and unfolded me,
and propelled me
through my little life.
I cannot see this Something.
Its silence is complete.
But I am a miracle walking,
a trillion cells all singing.
I'm in this land
by an unknown hand
and I have the wit to know it.

6

I don't know how much longer
I will walk this splendid Earth,
musing,
perceiving,
in wonder,
receiving,
and unfolding my human life.
However long it may be
I want to make the most of it.
I want to dive beneath
the crusty surface
to touch,
for just a moment,
the volcanic life of Being,
as It throws up my lovely world
and propels me through my days.

7

My world is at rest now.
The frenzied dance has stopped.
I'm in a cocoon of silence,
and stillness,
and brooding and gathering potential.
The night comes
to save us
from ourselves,
to stop us in our tracks,
to take us out of the chaos,
and still us into dream,
else we might never deepen,
dropping down to touch
the silent, black Ocean of Life.

8

Give me a moment to see myself
in context and with detachment,
without my hopes,
without my fear,
without the things
that I hold dear.
I want to see truly and deeply
why I am walking this earth,
why I have been sent here
to play my role
in a world that is clearly
not yet whole.
What do you want from me?
How can I find
the one I must be?
What is my part
in the unfolding plan,
and what should I do
with my brief life-span?

9

Once in a while
when I wake,
I'm filled
with expanding energy,
brimming with life-force sublime
that is bursting
with power to be.
I don't know
what to do with this.
I need a greater plan.
I need to use
this marvelous gift.
I need to find
a positive way
to hurl this energy
into the fray.

10

The fecund Earth is priming
to yield another Spring.
The sap is rising
toward the Sun,
the trees are blooming
one by one.
The world gets a brand new start,
and new life enters my aging heart.

11

The Cosmos is breathing Its life.
On the out-breath the world appears.
Unmoved,
untouched,
by Its own life magnificent,
It flexes Its creativity infinite.

12

The life-giving rain pours down,
water above,
water below,
the Earth opens up
with gratitude.
This rain will turn shortly
to flowers and grain,
and the life of our world
will renew again.

13

Blow me to the stars,
else what is this consciousness for?
We must be bigger than this.
I think that we were meant to soar,
to spin with the planets
and whirl with the suns,
to reach through the veils
of velvet night.
I know there is Majesty here.
It's simply beyond our sight.

14

I'm alive.
I'm breathing.
I'm conscious.
I'm perceiving.
Grace is raining upon me now.
I've been plucked from the night
so my soul could take flight
and swim in the Ocean of Life.
It's an interesting place,
this material space,
but I yearn to go home
where I really belong
to the wondrous Realm of Light.

15

I'm a creature of impulses
that come from the depths,
from the planets,
and God knows where else,
that move and propel me
through my life,
and make me into myself.
I'm watching to see
if these urges are me
or whether they come from Other.
I don't know what to believe.
Perhaps I am not in control here.
Perhaps my lifespan
is part of a plan
that is greater than
I can conceive.

16

From harmonic patterns
in the depths of Being
the things of the Cosmos
come forth.
My consciousness too
is a flowering
of patterns held in the fullness of space.
Mind and matter are coming
from the same invisible place.
Thrown up by the power
of unseeable Force,
reality emerges
from the Living Source.

17

Gratitude trumps fear,
and desolation
and despair
and loss.
To walk the Earth as a human
is a temporary thing.
We are here to regard the galaxies
and to dance with the planets' swing.
We are coming to know
that the Cosmic show
is our source, our origin.
In wonder, I've been here
for quite a while.
Now it is almost time to leave.
As I contemplate my coming departure
I simply refuse to grieve.
I want to die with a smile.

18

Livingness courses through me.
I tingle with its force.
My cells are alive
and my organs thrive
with the powers
of the unseen Source.
I'm conscious of my miracle.
I'm conscious of Living Space.
I'm conscious that every living thing
is held perfectly in place.
I'm grateful for this ride through time.
I've enjoyed my time on Earth.
It's been great to be a human.
It's been great to have a mind.

19

A brand new world
is rising into view,
a vision never seen,
with a new Cosmos too.
We must open our eyes.
We must open our hearts.
We must allow ourselves to change.
We are in the throes
of metamorphosis here.
We are seeing a brand-new view.
We are leaving our ancient past behind
We're becoming something new.

20

I am in a Living Field
of magical, living particles,
clustering and creating
the world of forms,
and unfolding an evolving Cosmos.
I am made of living particles,
thrown up from the depths of invisible Being.
My consciousness is the consciousness
of the Universe.
My life is the livingness of the Universe.
I am the Cosmos Itself,
in human form,
walking the Earth,
for just this brief span of time.

21

The Light and the Dark embrace
in streams of flowing flux,
locked together and inter-laced,
pulling the universe into form.
On Earth, the Light expands in the Spring
and the Dark recedes into night.
In Summer, the Light explodes itself
with expansion and life and warmth.
In Fall, the Light begins to dim
and the Dark rises in the Earth.
Silently and in stillness,
the Earth sinks into itself,
so potential and power can gather.
It's the way of the Sea of the Cosmos,
the Light and the Dark intertwined,
moving the one into the other,
alternating and enfolded,
cycling eternally.

22

In walking through my life
I have loved this splendid Earth,
with its clouds and flowers
and recurring Springs,
and its bottomless cornucopia
of new-born things.
I hope to continue my wonder,
to wake in the dawn
with a brimming heart,
to treat each day
as a brand-new start,
to linger awhile with Majesty,
before the clouds gather around me
to waft me into the galaxies.

23

The Cosmos has an interior,
invisible, living, aware,
filled with the blueprints
of Cosmic life
and bursting with potential.
Our minds have an interior too,
invisible, living, aware,
filled with the blueprints
of Cosmic life
and bursting with potential.
It's one and the same,
whatever its name,
these unseen patterns of life.
We can see the world
but can never see
its Source,
the living Interiority.

24

The middle of night.
I'm wide awake.
What shall I do with myself?
If left on its own
my mind will begin
to ring changes on endless problems.
Perhaps I can do better than that.
Perhaps I can,
with an effort of will,
open to touch Living Being.
Perhaps I can write
a little poem,
a spaceship of my mind,
then climb aboard and rev it up,
and blast off into the galaxies.

25

My consciousness
is the mind of the universe,
awake, alive, aware,
a Field of sensitivity
that is loaned to me
for just this very short span of time.
I can feel Its vastness.
I can feel Its depth.
I bathe in Its brilliant light.
Perhaps the purpose of this may be
to enable me to truly see
the meaning that is surrounding me
in the patterns of the Cosmos.

26

My world has stopped for the moment,
though the planets still swing and spin.
Here in the night,
under blazing starlight,
the vigor of Life is silent and still.
Life is building Itself for tomorrow,
and all the tomorrows to come.
It is fashioning Its vast magnificence
before my astonished eyes.
I feel Its dynamic potential
reaching up and through the skies.

27

Life is inexorable.
It presses ahead each moment
and floods the world
with Its energies
of birth and creation,
death and resurrection,
and endless renewal throughout.
At every second
the past drops away
and the future is coming to be.
At every second we humans face
the infinite Cosmic mystery.

28

I am a thing of particles,
living,
arranged in human form.
The universe beats my heart.
The universe pumps my lungs.
The universe floods my mind
with astounding consciousness.
I float in Cosmic livingness,
a living man in a Field of Life.
Life is blooming Itself
into me,
and through me,
and through the lovely Earth.
I am caught in miracle here.
I receive it all in wonder.

29

After swimming upstream for decades,
fighting the tide,
battling the water,
struggling with life,
there came a moment
when a thousand suns exploded,
showering me and penetrating me
with their booming spectral light.
Then I found myself swimming downstream
with the current at my back,
its force propelling and hurtling me
through time and space
at such a pace
that I scarcely could get my breath.
I have been waiting for this
and now it has finally come.
I bow my head in wonder.

30

A mystic is one who has,
and insists on having,
direct experience of the Cosmos,
never content to trace
the experience of another
from a few thousand years ago.
The mystic confronts Reality head-on,
in the present moment,
perceiving the invisible, sublime Reality that,
though It can never be seen,
throws up the ever-miraculous Cosmos.

31

I close my eyes.
I release my edges.
I search for Presence,
and I wait.
Then Something enters
my waiting heart
and fires my body's inside.
I am flooded throughout with ecstasy.
I hear the galaxies' distant thunder.
I am lifted aloft on wings of wonder.

32

Everywhere is the center
of the conscious, mysterious Sea.
The Field is living throughout.
New life can emerge,
without a doubt,
at every single point.
Our consciousness too
is a center of life,
a marvelous, focused store
of coherence,
and perception,
and integration,
and sublime Being, and more.
We fit perfectly into the world.
We are at its very core.

33

Gather Your Presence around me.
Fire my every nerve with bliss.
Lift me out of this blackest place,
and banish all my fears.
Don't leave me alone like this.
I'm small,
I'm weak,
I'm vulnerable.
I cannot do it on my own.
I open my heart
and all my cells.
To You, I turn my face.
I'm waiting here,
expectantly,
for You to fill this empty space.

34

What shall I do
with my precious life?
What task is worth my time?
I'm here for a day,
but there is no way
I can measure up to the task.
Give me a clue
of what to do
to join in Your sacred dance.
I'm willing to apply myself
if only I'm given a chance.

35

Why is it that,
when I wake sometimes,
I'm lost in desolation?
My heart is closed.
My world is small.
My prospects seem so few.
I cannot do the simplest things
to expand into
a deeper view.
I should know by now
how to cope with this,
this emptiness enshrined.
But I don't know how
to rouse myself
to touch Your life sublime.

36

As I write,
I feel Your Presence
as it enters my empty heart.
My nerves begin to tingle
with Your infinite energy.
I'm lifted into
a brand new start,
and richness envelops me.
You are always there,
just waiting for me,
if I'll only take
and shake myself
and allow myself to wake.

37

The veils of my ego
close round me,
foreclosing the miracles
that I can see.
I become smaller.
My world becomes smaller.
My life becomes greyer
and overwhelmingly mundane.
Yesterday the veils flew open,
and I could suddenly see
the being that I might become,
the being that I might be.
Each day is a separate experience.
I change from hour to hour.
I'm fighting the veils
and trying to expand.
Is it too much to ask
that You give me a hand?

38

The unadorned Truth shines forth
with a radiant, spectral light.
Reality lies simmering below
the level of our sight.
Presence around us
cannot be seen,
or tasted,
or touched,
or smelled.
We must sensitize ourselves
to sense It
with our nerves and with our cells.
It is waiting there now
for us.
It is waiting for us
to grow up.
We are learning to reach
with our bodies
toward the touch
of Its outstretched hand.

39

When I turn my head
and try to see
the Presence that is
surrounding me,
there appears to be
nothing there.
Yet, I feel You
in my heart.
I know You're here
in this room,
firing my mind,
and beating my heart,
and sending me
my every breath.
You're making it possible
for me to be,
and I can clearly see
that as I write,
in every moment,
Your grace is raining
upon me.

40

Sometimes,
when the light
is right,
I see through the crust of the world.
I'm enveloped
in moments of wonder,
in the richness
of Living Light,
and I touch
the deep realities
that lie just beyond my sight.
My heart fills up
and I can see
the Life that stretches
in every direction
and reaches into infinity.

41

Give me a moment of Your time.
Touch me in my heart.
Lift my flagging spirits,
and give me a brand-new start.
I'm empty today
and there is no way
I can do this for myself.
I arrange myself.
I open myself,
and I'm waiting,
waiting,
waiting.

42

The veils are tight around me.
They close my eyes.
They shrink my mind.
I find it impossible to see
the beauty of the world.
Yet, I know it is still there.
This is all inside me.
I will be still and silent,
and wait until I
can once again see
the miracle that it is
to be.

43

I close my eyes.
I release my edges.
I open my heart.
I relax my body.
I search for Presence
in the space around.
I wait for Your touch,
but now I see
that it's really not up to me.

44

I touch Your depth,
and I can see
that it stretches down
to infinity.
How small I am.
How limited I am.
I'm stunned and awed
by Your immensity.
I bow to You.
I bow to You.

45

Every moment that I am alive
and walking this splendid Earth
is a gift of great immensity.
My moods go up,
my moods go down,
and I'm caught in life's intensity.
But, through it all
I can clearly see
the on-going gift
that is raining on me.
In wonder,
I am allowed to be.

46

From separateness,
alone in a hard world,
I break through
into Immensity.
The veils are lifted.
My eyes are opened,
and my heart expands
into infinity.

47

Like a hummingbird,
I'm in search
of the sweetest nectar,
always hidden
deep down things.
In constant motion,
I flit from flower to flower,
from thing to thing,
looking desperately
for the one core truth
that will lay bare
the heart of Reality,
reveal the depths,
and bring me rest.

48

Early blue morning.
The world is holding its breath,
waiting for the Sun to rise
and illuminate the skies
with light,
and warmth,
and life.
The birds will wax ecstatic,
in praise,
and joy,
and welcome,
as the promise of a new day,
a day in the life of Earth,
miraculously dawns.

49

This moment
I am suffused
with richness and joy,
and hope and life,
and Being's electric touch.
I am lit inside
with Living Light.
My nerves are tingling
with Being's might.
I feel myself fully alive.
Occasionally, humans can have this.
I bow my head in gratitude.

50

Who creates?
Not me.
I'm only here to be
the fingers for the Powers
that I can never see,
Powers that are presently
turning the world
and beating my heart,
and spinning the galaxy.

51

I seem to be invisible
to this spinning, hectic world.
I write my poems.
I live my life.
I pass from day to day.
What is this need
to have applause?
What difference does it make?
What value could I glean
from the experience of being seen?
I think that I will always be
a study in obscurity.
Get over it.

52

I want to dive,
headlong,
down into depth and meaning,
and swim in the
Sea of Reality.
I want to touch
the Invisible One.
I want to view
the Source of my life
and the genesis
of billions of worlds.
I want to see,
in some small way,
Divinity unfurled.

53

The culture is the "World of Lies,"
pandering to the trivial and perverse,
and soaked in self-regard.
Its instructions to us are false.
Leave behind
this realm of the blind,
and turn your face to the Sun.
We are wholly, in fact, a miracle
waiting to realize ourselves.

54

Minute by minute
I am lit by Life.
Minute by minute
I am moving toward death.
Now I can clearly see
that my fate will surely be
to become a part
of the Cosmic Sea.
Get ready for the journey.

55

How can I open myself to space?
How can I touch the Living Void?
I cannot see
what is throwing up me,
but I can feel It in the air.
There is Livingness all around me.
I am carried and sustained right now
by a living Cosmic Sea.
How can I capture Infinity?

56

I write these poems
one at a time,
a wisp of the Cosmos
enfolded in rhyme,
trying to pierce
the veil of the world,
and touch Livingness beneath,
trying to deepen,
trying to broaden,
to burst through the bounds
of my little self,
to touch the invisible Presence
that is throwing up our world.

57

I thought I was alone here,
vulnerable,
threatened,
unsupported.
Then I encountered Being,
invisible,
mysterious,
alive.
I opened to Its embrace,
Its intimacy,
Its warmth,
Its support.
Now Being is as close
as the pulse in my throat.

58

Every day of my life
is a separate gift.
My first job is to
accept the gift
with consciousness.
My second job is
not to spoil the gift
with fear.

59

I am irradiated,
moment to moment,
with the depth,
meaning,
and sacredness
of Being.
I am a channel
for the Mystery
to come through.

60

Chaos on the right.
Chaos on the left.
In seeking my happiness
I'm often left bereft.
Life slips through my fingers.
I need a solid pier,
to handle my confusion,
to handle all my fear.
Being is the North Star.
Turn your face to the darkened sky.
Ground yourself in Being
and give It a serious try.

61

Beneath the world of night
lies a realm of Living Light.
Radiance all around us.
Behind the Cosmic show
and under the material crust,
the Earth of Light is shining
with a spectral, self-luminous glow.

62

We spend our lives
trying to figure out
how to get value
and be O.K.
What if we're already there?
What if value was conferred on us
at the moment of our birth?
We have been plucked
from the Void
to walk this splendid Earth
as a human being
for just a short span of time,
the latest model
of this marvelous creature,
fifteen billion years
in the making,
now the Cosmos
in human form.
This is our value.

63

How could I have managed
to sleep through all those years?
I thought I was awake,
alive,
and expanding my life,
but I see now
that I was sleeping,
unconscious of the grandeur
and mystery surrounding
and fueling my every thought.
What a waste!
I have walked the Earth for decades,
without eyes,
without ears,
without perceiving or feeling
the harmonies of the spheres.

64

Facing the night sky,
we confront infinity.
Mystery is its name.
Livingness is its game.
It has given birth
to we beings on Earth,
and brought us from the Void,
to dance the frenzied
dream of life,
and to gaze above
in wonder and in awe.

65

We are caught and held suspended
between the order of the Cosmos
and the chaos of the Earth,
reaching,
yearning,
stretching,
to penetrate the chaos,
and touch the orchestration
of the Livingness beneath.

66

We are searching for a vision
to explain why we are here,
to justify our pain,
to justify our fear.
We feel our evolution
unfolding as we speak.
The world is changing.
We are changing.
Change is now a frenzied thing.
Caught in metamorphosis,
we wonder where it may lead.
Where are we going?
Why are we here,
and what does the Cosmos need?

67

Beyond gravity,
beyond the mechanical pull
of material and mass,
a force is operating
to bring things together.
The result is new life,
a fresh surge in the unfolding
of mysterious, invisible Being.
All around us, silently,
the universe is blooming Itself,
intent on expressing Its
own sublime, generative nature.
We walk the Earth today,
emerging from the Source,
brought into life
to dance our dance
as products of
this merging force.

68

Wonder is not a trivial thing.
It opens our eyes.
It opens our hearts,
so that we may see,
with clarity,
the splendor of our life.
It lifts us up to miracles
that lap unceasingly
in and around our little selves.
It ends our state of sleep,
and charges our cells with livingness.
Turn toward your wonder now.
Lose yourself in awe.
Open to the living Cosmos
and deepen your precious life.

69

I wait
for the touch of Your wonder,
to bring me to life
and open my eyes,
and fire my heart with grace.
Then I can be truly alive.
And I know it is true,
in the scheme of things,
with the consciousness that wonder brings,
that wonder is waiting on me,
to slow down,
to look within,
to see things truly and deeply,
to open to the Majesty
in which I ceaselessly swim.

70

This day that is waiting to dawn
has unlimited potential gifts.
It can shower me with riches
or it can be barren and dry.
It's all up to me.
It depends on whether
I can see
beneath the crust of matter.
It depends on whether
I can feel
the invisible life
of the Cosmic Sea.
It depends on whether
I can open
myself to Life's divinity.
It's all up to me.
It's all up to me.

71

Sometimes I see that I have kept
myself from feeling Your infinite depth.
I must work on myself
to refine my soul.
I must sensitize myself
so that I can see,
and fully be,
a participant in divinity.

72

Burgeoning creativity
is blooming all around me.
The universe is in full flower,
in perpetuity.
Invisible Being unfolds Itself,
and expresses Itself,
and evolves Itself,
always gracefully.
Before our astonished eyes,
It unfurls Its vast divinity,
always effortlessly.

73

I am along for the ride.
I'd like to think I'm instrumental.
I'd like to think
that I can be
the power that is unfolding me,
but I know this is not the case.
I am ensconced in Vastness,
unfurling Its gifts at such a pace,
in a rich, magnificent tapestry,
that I can only watch breathlessly
as It unfolds my life.
I am most certainly,
most definitely,
just along for the ride.

74

There is richness here
that I cannot see,
but I feel it with my cells.
There is potential here
that's unexpressed
in the space that's
all around me.
There is Livingness waiting
to unfold Itself.
The future is waiting to be.

75

What is the deepest thing
that I can touch,
my highest capacity?
What can I see
of Divinity
that is surrounding and enfolding me?
How can I amp up and encourage
my developing sensitivity?
I am a work in progress.
Being is so vast and deep
and so profoundly Other
that It always will remain beyond.
But, now and then,
if I quietly wait,
I can get a tiny glimpse.
It is enough.

76

The body connects us to Being.
The mind is no good here.
We reach toward the Source,
the invisible Force,
with our talented billions of cells.
If you open yourself and wait,
and sense your body's inside,
you may feel a flow of ecstasy
that is lighting up your self.
This is the feeling of Being,
this ecstasy that you sense.
Wake up your body and open your field.
Touch Being as It is unfurled.
Expand your experience of being alive
and enter a brand-new world.

77

The universe is breathing us
in and out,
in our hearts,
in our lungs,
in our days and nights.
We ceaselessly shift
from pole to pole,
moving in an eternal pulse,
an eternal oscillation,
that drives our precious livingness.

78

The universe knew we were coming.
Through billions of years
of exploding stars,
It had us in mind
all of that time.
It made the conditions perfect
to bring us to where we are now,
a conscious ape,
under the Sun,
now awake and aware
that the Cosmos is one.
Now we are here,
fully formed,
and ready to play our role
in unfolding, mysterious Cosmic life,
in the emerging, magnificent whole.
Lift your eyes
to the skies above
and let yourself mentally fly.
Dance the dance of Oneness now.
As you whirl in place
let yourself sing out:
"I have come from the world of men,
to dance my part in the cavalcade.
I have come to fulfill my destiny.
Let the Cosmic games begin!"